KU-149-478

Did You Know?

MANCHESTER

A MISCELLANY

Compiled by Julia Skinner

With a particular reference to the work of Clive Hardy

THE FRANCIS FRITH COLLECTION

www.francisfrith.com

Based on a book first published in the United Kingdom in 2005 by The Francis Frith Collection®

Hardback edition published in 2012 ISBN: 978-1-84589-414-6

Text and Design copyright The Francis Frith Collection®
Photographs copyright The Francis Frith Collection® except where indicated.

The Frith® photographs and the Frith® logo are reproduced under licence from Heritage Photographic Resources Ltd, the owners of the Frith® archive and trademarks.
'The Francis Frith Collection', 'Francis Frith' and 'Frith' are registered trademarks of Heritage Photographic Resources Ltd.

All rights reserved. No photograph in this publication may be sold to a third party other than in the original form of this publication, or framed for sale to a third party. No parts of this publication may be reproduced, stored in a retrieval system, or transmitted, in any form, or by any means, electronic, mechanical, photocopying, recording or otherwise, without the prior permission of the publishers and copyright holder.

British Library Cataloguing in Publication Data

Did You Know? Manchester - A Miscellany
Compiled by Julia Skinner
With particular reference to the work of Clive Hardy

The Francis Frith Collection
Oakley Business Park,
Wylye Road, Dinton,
Wiltshire SP3 5EU
Tel: +44 (0) 1722 716 376
Email: info@francisfrith.co.uk
www.francisfrith.com

Printed and bound in Malaysia

Front Cover: **MANCHESTER, MARKET STREET 1889** 21899p

The colour-tinting is for illustrative purposes only, and is not intended to be historically accurate

AS WITH ANY HISTORICAL DATABASE, THE FRANCIS FRITH ARCHIVE IS CONSTANTLY BEING CORRECTED AND IMPROVED, AND THE PUBLISHERS WOULD WELCOME INFORMATION ON OMISSIONS OR INACCURACIES

CONTENTS

INTRODUCTION

The busy modern city of Manchester stands on historic foundations.
It was the site of the Roman Mamucium, a camp built by Agricola's
legions on the banks of the River Irwell in AD 79, on their way from
Chester to York. It was weaving, first of woollen goods and then
of cotton, which brought Manchester its 19th-century power and
glory, but the city's weaving tradition dates back to Flemish weavers
introduced by Edward III in the 14th century. However, Manchester was
little more than a market town until the Industrial Revolution made it
the main trading centre for Lancashire cotton.

Soon Manchester was known as 'Cottonopolis', and was at the hub
of the expanding cotton trade. Proximity to coal supplies and an ideal
climate for textile work helped its development; the damp climate
prevented the cotton thread from splitting when being spun. It was
the world's first truly industrial city, a role symbolised by the first
commercial use of a steam engine in 1783, at Richard Arkwright's
cotton spinning factory. This rapid expansion and population growth
brought its own problems: Alexis de Tocqueville called Manchester a
'foul drain' from which 'the greatest stream of industry flows out to
fertilize the whole world'. A vivid (but possibly exaggerated) description
of Manchester at this time was also written by Engels in 'The Condition
of the Working Class in England' (1845). As Manchester grew in the
19th century it had to break away from the strong influence of Salford,
which ruled over the ancient 'hundred' and held all the administrative
power in the area. Manchester's influence increased by the fact that
the parish church was situated in its area; after the church was turned
into a Collegiate Church, Manchester became the centre of learning
and law-making in the area.

'The fastest growing town in England' was how Manchester was described 250 years ago. There seemed to be a determination in the minds of the burghers and leading citizens to make something of the place, to push forward this small town in north-west England and stamp its name not just on the rest of the country, but on the world. They succeeded, and in the years that followed Manchester became the place where the first canal system was started, passenger railways were born, and plans for a great ship canal were hatched – and in more recent times it was the birthplace of the modern computer. Manchester's story is full of colourful characters and events, of which this book can only give a glimpse.

MANCHESTER, MARKET STREET 1889 21899

MANCHESTER DIALECT WORDS AND PHRASES

'A bally ann meal' - a meal thrown together from whatever is available.

'b'art' or *'beawt'* - without.

'Bidding' - an invitation to a funeral.

'Bobber' - the person who woke people up for work before the days of alarm clocks. Bobbers carried long poles, with which they knocked on windows as they passed along the streets.

'Boggart' - a ghost or spirit, especially those which lived in holes.

'Chitty' - a young girl or lass, as in 'a chit of a girl'.

'Claggy' - sticky, can be used to describe dough, mud or sticky weather.

'Clough' - a steep-sided valley.

'Delph' - a quarry or excavation.

'Fettle' - to mend, or repair.

'Hippins' - babies' nappies.

'Keks' - trousers.

'Mawkin' - dirty or shabby.

'Motty' - a small amount of money.

'Petty' - an outdoor toilet.

'Reasty' or *'resty'* - rotten, gone off (as of food).

'Sen' - self, as in mi-sen (myself).

'Sennit' - a week (seven nights).

'Skrike' - to cry out or shriek.

'Spun up for bobbins' - nothing to do.

'Yammer' - to want something badly.

HAUNTED MANCHESTER

The Western Hotel in Alexandra Road, Moss Side is believed to be haunted by the ghost of a former cellarman, who wears a grey sweater, has dark hair, and appears to be a man in his thirties. He has been seen in several locations but is usually spotted in the cellars, accompanied by a drop in temperature, and vanishes after a few seconds.

An old bus from Stockport that is now on show in the Manchester Transport Museum is believed to be haunted, and in fact this was a belief that was current amongst the bus crews even when the bus was operating, from 1952 to 1969. The ghost of a young boy, dressed in a 1950s-style pullover and shorts, was seen during restoration, and this has also been seen by visitors. An artist with no knowledge of the ghost story who was commissioned to draw the bus added the face of a young boy at an upper window. Investigation revealed that the bus was once involved in an accident at Reddish, in which a young boy was killed.

In the 19th century the area of the Old Church, which is now Manchester Cathedral, was believed to be haunted by the ghost of a headless dog.

Dixon Green Labour Club, Farnworth, was built on the site of an old manor house, and a ghost, known as the Blue Lady, has been seen and heard in the club on several occasions.

MANCHESTER MISCELLANY

Peel Park opened in 1846 and is named in honour of Prime Minister Sir Robert Peel. He not only secured government funding for the park, but made a generous donation himself. In the park was Lark Hill, a mansion built in 1790 and formerly the home of Colonel Ackers of the Manchester & Salford Volunteers. In January 1850 Lark Hill became Britain's first totally free public library. The original house was demolished in 1937.

Though called Manchester Docks, most of the port was in fact in Salford; only the Pomona wharves, which handled coastal vessels and short sea routes, were in Manchester. No 9 Dock, the largest of all the docks, was built on land purchased from the Manchester Racecourse Co, and was officially opened by King Edward VII and Queen Alexandra on 13 July 1905. The withdrawal of container traffic spelt the end for Manchester, and by the early 1980s the docks had been flattened in readiness for redevelopment, both for residential and leisure purposes.

The triangular-shaped Victoria Buildings was erected by the corporation in the late 1880s, occupying an area of land bounded by Deansgate, Victoria Street and St Mary's Gate. The corporation laid a circuit of tracks around the building which in-bound trams followed. This did away with the need to turn the trams, for by completing the circuit they would automatically be facing in the right direction for the next outward trip.

Did You Know?
MANCHESTER
A MISCELLANY

MANCHESTER, FROM THE VICTORIA HOTEL 1889 21884

At the centre bottom of the photograph above is the statue of Oliver Cromwell by Matthew Noble, in its original position; it is now in Wythenshawe Park, minus its sword. The statue was conceived, commissioned and paid for by Thomas Goadsby, mayor of Manchester. It was presented to the city by Mrs Abel Heywood in memory of Thomas Goadsby, who had been her first husband. She wanted it sited on the banks of the Irwell because Thomas had saved her life here when her father's boat, the 'Emma', capsized; many people were drowned in the tragedy. It was the first large-scale statue of Cromwell to be raised in the open anywhere in England.

Dedicated to the Glorious Virgin and the holy martyrs St Denis and St George, Manchester's cathedral was originally built as a collegiate church by Thomas, Lord de la Warre, in the 15th century. It was the church's first warden, John Huntingdon, who built the choir; his successor added the nave, and the third warden widened the choir and added the clerestory. During restoration work in the 1880s some fragments of Saxon masonry were unearthed.

The Royal Exchange in Manchester was where the Lancashire cotton industry did business with the world. The words around the great dome in the centre of the building were: 'A good name is rather to be chosen than great riches, and loving favour rather than silver and gold'.

MANCHESTER, THE SHIP CANAL 1895 36396

MANCHESTER, THE SHIP CANAL, GRAIN ELEVATORS c1965 M21502

This photograph was taken several years before the opening of the container terminal on North No 9 Dock. At the head of the dock can be seen the large No 2 grain elevator; later this was so much trouble to pull down that it took nearly three months before it was cleared away. There had been a No 1 grain elevator on Trafford Wharf, but this had been hit by an incendiary bomb during the Second World War, and after months of burning and smouldering, because it was full of grain, it was finally pulled down. Containerisation traffic led Manchester Liners to restructure their fleet. Some ships, such as 'Manchester Progress' (8,176grt) were converted to cellular containerships, and new ships were ordered, such as 'Manchester Challenge' (12,000grt) and her sisters 'Manchester Courage' and 'Manchester Concorde'.

Manchester's Free Trade Hall is the home of one of the country's leading orchestras, the Hallé, founded in 1858 by Sir Charles Hallé. Its principal conductors have included Hans Richter and Sir John Barbirolli.

> The Liverpool to Manchester Railway opened in 1830 and was the world's first commercially successful line. It was built by George Stephenson (1781-1848) whose locomotive 'Rocket' heralded the railway age.

There is a series of twelve murals in the Town Hall by the Pre Raphaelite artist Ford Madox Brown, depicting events in the city's history; one of them shows the Manchester schoolmaster John Dalton collecting marsh gases. His research provided the first insight into the understanding of atomic matter.

MANCHESTER, THE EXHIBITION STATION 1887 21904

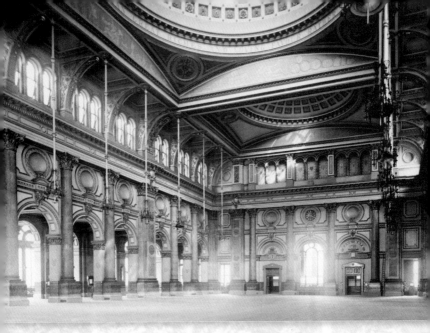

MANCHESTER, THE ROYAL EXCHANGE, THE GREAT HALL 1885 18262

This was dubbed 'the largest room in the world'. It was 4,405 square yards in area, and 96 feet high, 125 feet high to the central dome. The floor of the Royal Exchange was the scene of frantic activity on Tuesdays and Fridays, when at the hour of High Exchange anything up to 1,100 men would gather here and shout at one another, and many a fortune was made or lost. Though the floor appeared chaotic to the outsider, it was in fact well organised; there were numbers on the posts running down the hall, and letters on the posts running across the hall, so that businesses could co-ordinate where to meet in such a busy and packed room. Buyers, agents, manufacturers and merchants had their regular places. Those who did their business here would know where to find the Blackburn cotton manufacturers, or the Oldham cotton spinners, as well as cotton brokers, agents for the Indian and Chinese markets, and machinery manufacturers.

From a single tram route of a couple of miles in length in 1877, Manchester's tram network had over 20 miles of track by the end of 1881. Though the Corporation built, owned and maintained the tramway, the running of services was leased to the Manchester Suburban Tramways Co who paid between £300 and £450 a year per track mile.

In 1866 the Corporation decided that the design for their Town Hall should be by open competition, a normal 19th-century practice for civic buildings. There were 130 entries, the winner being Alfred Waterhouse. The Town Hall covered a site of nearly two acres; building began in 1868 and was also completed in 1877 at a cost of about £1 million.

MANCHESTER, THE TOWN HALL 1895 36380

Did You Know?
MANCHESTER
A MISCELLANY

MANCHESTER, THE GRAND HOTEL c1885 18290

Costing over £130,000 to build and opened in July 1864, Manchester's Assize Court was a blend of Early English and Victorian Gothic. Behind the courts was the county prison, housing 800 male and 600 female prisoners. The prison was for its day a state-of-the-art secure establishment, with wings radiating out from a central block.

In 1824 the Royal Manchester Institution chose the design of Charles Barry (1795-1860) for their new headquarters in Mosley Street. The new building opened in 1834, but was taken over by Manchester Corporation in 1882, on the understanding that they spent £2,000 per year buying works of art, and became the City Art Gallery. Manchester's City Art Gallery is famous for its collection of paintings, specialising in the development of English art from the 16th century to the present day.

There was a settlement in the Manchester area in Anglo-Saxon times, called Mamecaster. The Domesday Book of 1086 records St Mary's Church, which probably stood on the site of the present cathedral.

MANCHESTER, ST ANNE'S SQUARE AND THE CHURCH 1886 18265

On the grave of John Peters, a drunken cobbler of Manchester:

> Enclosed within this narrow stall
> Lies one who was a friend to *awl*.
> He saved bad *soles* from getting worse,
> But damned his own without remorse,
> And though a drunken life he passed,
> Yet saved his *sole*, by *mending at the last*.

The heart of Manchester was always its parish church, which became a cathedral in 1847; it contains some fine 16th-century carved woodwork.

Two Mancunians, Captain Sir John Alcock and Sir Arthur Whitten Brown, were the first men to fly the Atlantic Ocean, in 1919.

The Manchester Regiment Chapel (formerly the Derby Chapel) in the cathedral was badly damaged by enemy bombing in the Second World War. It now has a modern stained glass window, designed in wonderful shades of reds and oranges to depict the flames of the bombing.

MANCHESTER, THE CATHEDRAL 1899 43334

This extract is from the 'Vicar's Notes' in the parish magazine of
All Saints' Church, Manchester, in 1936:
'I shall be away from the parish attending the Diocesan Clergy

School from 21-24 April. It will be convenient if parishioners will abstain from arranging to be buried, or from making other calls on me during this time.'

MANCHESTER, ALBERT MEMORIAL SQUARE 1892 30382

MANCHESTER, THE CATHEDRAL CHOIR c1885 18250

The Lady Chapel of Manchester Cathedral is behind the high altar; unfortunately all the lovely stained glass seen in the photograph on page 20 was blown out in December 1940 when the cathedral was bombed. The rebuilding took nearly 20 years, and the craftsmen tried to put only the best and finest materials back into Manchester's chief house of God. 192 new traceried panels were fitted to the ancient beams of the choir roof. Thousands of pieces of new wood had to be let into the elaborate canopies of the choir stalls seen here. Most of these stalls had been put here by Sir James Stanley in 1513. He was brother to the man who married the mother of Henry VII, and the family enjoyed power and influence for centuries later.

After the Municipal Corporation Act had been passed in 1835 many Lancashire towns had started down the road to becoming boroughs, but Manchester did not become a corporation until 1838. There had been some unrest at the way Manchester had been managed, and it was Richard Cobden who urged Mancunians to 'put an end to this thing' and have a council elected by the people. The Charter of Incorporation of the Borough of Manchester was granted by Queen Victoria on 23 October 1838; after much debate, and accusations of vote rigging and ballot fixing, Manchester was given the right to set aside the self-elected officials and hold the first municipal election.

After becoming a borough in its own right in 1838, the Charter which made Manchester a city was granted on 29 March 1853; it had risen from a suburb of Salford to a city in only fifteen years.

MANCHESTER
A MISCELLANY
Did You Know?

In the 19th century the rivalry between Liverpool and Manchester was such that advisors to Queen Victoria said that the honour of the title of Lord Mayor could not be given to one city and not the other. At exactly 11am on 3 August 1893, one of Queen Victoria's ministers entered the office of both Liverpool's and Manchester's mayor and laid before each Her Majesty's permission to the title of Lord Mayor; thus neither could claim a victory over the other.

The photograph on page 23 shows the choir screen and the organ above it. The organ in Manchester Cathedral was one of the very best in the country and technically superb, ranking tenth in Great Britain. It was completely destroyed during the blitz of the Second World War, and could not be saved.

Originally the area of St Anne's Square was called Acres Field, and it was here that the Manchester Fair was held on the eve, day and morrow of St Matthew, September 20-22. It was here that woollen fairs and cattle markets were held, until the square became too developed; then the fairs moved down to Castlefields. In 1706 the square was laid out in plots, and building started. The church was paid for by Lady Ann Bland, the last of the Mosley family, and opened in 1709.

Emmeline Pankhurst was born in Manchester in 1858. She founded the Women's Franchise League in 1889, and then, with her daughter Christabel, the Women's Social and Political Union in 1903, initiating the militant Suffragette campaign. She was frequently arrested and imprisoned during her long campaign to win women the right to vote. Her home at 96 Nelson Street still stands.

Manchester's Trafford Park was the world's first industrial park.

MANCHESTER, OLD TRAFFORD 1897 39050

This photograph shows the stand of the Lancashire Cricket Ground, called Old Trafford, as it looked over a century ago. 50 years earlier, the Manchester Cricket Club took over the Clifford cricket ground, situated between Chester Road and Talbot Road. The club moved across the road to Old Trafford in 1857. The first game on this new ground was against the Liverpool Gentlemen, which Manchester won. In 1864 it was decided to form a County Club, and Lancashire Cricket Club was born. The stand shown here was built in 1884 of red brick at a cost of £9,033 (£2,000 more than the estimate). It was bombed in the Second World War, and has now been added to and modernised out of all recognition.

The Royal Infirmary, seen in the photograph below, with its high dome and clock face, lords it over Piccadilly. The hospital opened in 1775; the portico entrance nearest the camera in this photograph was the front of a Mental Asylum, which was incorporated into the building. A public bath house was also part of the block; as well as serving the people of the back streets around Piccadilly, it meant that patients could be given a bath before entering the hospital. The cabs in the photograph include examples of the famous hansom cab, designed and built by Charles Hansom of Manchester.

MANCHESTER, THE ROYAL INFIRMARY c1885 18256

The bronze statue of John Cobden in the middle of St Anne's Square was paid for by public subscription and was presented to the town in 1867 by the President of the Anti-Corn Law League. It is by Marshall Wood, and originally stood where the Boer War

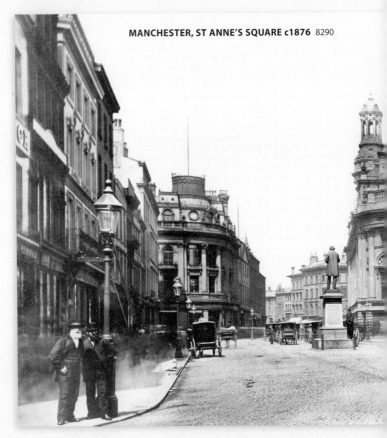

MANCHESTER, ST ANNE'S SQUARE c1876 8290

Memorial is today. Richard Cobden, like his colleague John Bright, whose statue is in Albert Square, was a supporter of Free Trade and an opponent of the Corn Laws, which banned the import of cheap foreign wheat.

The marble statue of John Bright, by A Bruce Joy, was unveiled in Albert Square on 12 October 1891 by Lord Derby. John Bright, with his close associate Cobden, was a passionate believer in free trade. His gift of oratory enabled him to deliver moving speeches with sincerity and passion. He worked tirelessly for the repeal of the Corn Laws, which came about in 1846. John Bright was elected MP for Manchester in 1847, but his outspoken opposition to the Crimean War and his Quaker moral sense of duty turned Manchester people against him. When he stood as MP for Manchester in 1857 he was rejected, and an effigy of him was burnt in the street.

What is now a household name, Brooke Bond & Co, was a Manchester firm of tea and coffee importers founded by Samuel Brooke.

The Victoria Buildings were built in the late 1880s and were named in honour of Queen Victoria's 50 years on the throne. The Victoria Buildings, which dominated the cathedral end of Deansgate, included 28 shops, 88 offices and 48 cellars, as well as a 231-roomed hotel. The power for the lifts was provided by a hydraulic water-power system that came directly from the pump house situated on Quay Street, by the River Irwell, where the water came from.

The unique Barton Swing Aqueduct was designed by Edward Leader Williams to carry the Bridgewater Canal over the Manchester Ship Canal. The requirement was that the aqueduct had to be capable of being swung clear whilst full of water, so as not to interfere with shipping movements on the Ship Canal.

MANCHESTER, THE JOHN BRIGHT STATUE 1892 30383

On Tuesday 1 September 1908 a large crowd gathered in Piccadilly to watch about 100 patients being moved out of the Infirmary (the domed building left of the photograph on page 31). Horse-drawn ambulances, taxi cabs, flat wagons and even a horse-bus were used to convey the patients to the new Royal Infirmary on Oxford Road. Only one patient was left behind because he was too ill to move. The main buildings of the old infirmary were soon demolished, but the Wash House remained, as did part of the Asylum, which was used as a reference library before the Central Library was built.

BARTON UPON IRWELL, BARTON AQUEDUCT 1894 33693

The Manchester Ship Canal was opened in 1894, as a way of shipping goods out directly from Manchester, thus avoiding the costs of railway transport and Liverpool's high dock charges. One Manchester merchant said that when sending a ton of goods from Manchester to Australia it was costing him more for the journey to Liverpool and on to the ship than for the rest of the trip to the customer. The answer came from a man called Daniel Adamson, who called a meeting of all the best minds and mayors around Manchester to discuss a plan 'to bring the sea to Manchester'. One of the men he invited was Marshall Stevens, who was made head of the committee to steer the plans through Parliament - the Manchester Ship Canal bill got through Parliament at its third attempt. When the Ship Canal opened, making the city a port 36 miles from the sea, the traffic was a mixed bag of sailing ships, steam ships and motor vessels. Despite the present-day lack of commercial traffic, the Canal is still there; 70,000 gallons of water an hour on average flow down the Canal, and it needs to be dredged regularly and kept in good order to prevent flooding.

MANCHESTER, ST ANNE'S SQUARE, THE CAB RANK 1885 18263

The area nearest the camera in the photograph above was once the graveyard for St Ann's Church. As you walk the area today it is hard to imagine how many former citizens rest under the concrete and paving stones. Manchester's first election for Members of Parliament was held in St Anne's Square, and after a day of speech-making Philips and Poulett were duly elected.

Portland Street was known as the street of warehouses. In 1845 this street had been nothing more than a dirt track with some third-rate shops. By 1895 businesses in Portland Street included A & S Henry (Importers), the famous S & J Watts & Co, and Sam Mendel, a rope and twine manufacturer who lived at Manley Park, Chorlton.

The name Humphrey Chetham and his charitable work is synonymous with Manchester's history. When he died in 1653 Humphrey Chetham had already started the work of educating the 'sons of honest, industrious and painful parents.' His will left money to make sure that the work continued, and in 1656 Chetham College opened. Today the college is still a vibrant place of learning, and open to a much wider range of pupils than Humphrey Chetham ever dreamed of.

The statue of Cromwell, seen below in the middle of the photograph, was for many years nicknamed 'the pedestrian's friend' as it gave a refuge to people crossing the busy street.

MANCHESTER, THE VICTORIA HOTEL 1889 21916

The area from the Duke of Wellington statue to Market Street was once a large ornamental pond, complete with fountains, which had delighted Queen Victoria and Prince Albert when they visited

Manchester in 1840; before that, the area was called the 'dawb holes'; clay was taken from here to make local bricks. At the time of this photograph it was newly laid out and paved.

MANCHESTER, PICCADILLY 1889 22158

CHETHAM COLLEGE, HUMPHREY CHETHAM'S ROOM 1889 22259

This is the reading room of Chetham College's library. This room has been a favourite of many famous people; in here, Karl Marx and Frederick Engels spent many hours philosophising on the class struggle, and discussing economic and political theories. Engels had been sent to Manchester to manage a branch of his father's cotton firm; Marx came to Manchester in 1845 to visit his friend and colleague. Engels was appalled at the living and working conditions of the people who were creating the wealth of the city. He published his findings in 'The Condition of the Working Class in England' in Germany in 1845; in that year he also began his collaboration with Marx which culminated in 'The Communist Manifesto' (1848).

The gothic pile of the Assize Court on Great Ducie Street opened in 1864, when Manchester held its first Assize Session there. Alfred Waterhouse, who designed Manchester's Town Hall, was given the job of providing a court building to match the city's growing importance. It was once said that Waterhouse had designed for all classes of Mancunians, with the Assizes, the Refuge Assurance Building, the Town Hall and the Jail all in his portfolio. This building was bombed during the Second World War and could not be saved.

MANCHESTER, THE ASSIZE COURT 1886 18251

Manchester's Central Library was opened by King George V in 1934, and it was then the largest public library in the country. The Cenotaph nearby was built to a design by Sir Edward Lutyens; it is similar to the one in Whitehall, and it is sited where St Peter's Church once stood. There had been a large crypt in the church where over 2,500 of Manchester's citizens were laid to rest, because there was no graveyard. This was sealed and built over because of the problems of moving the collapsing coffins, and skeletons. So, when you stand on the platform to catch a tram, spare a thought for the 2,500 Mancunians resting below.

The Manchester merchant John Owen, who died in 1846, made a fortune by hard work and honest dealing. He left the then considerable sum of £100,000 to form a college, where all faiths and denominations would be admitted. At first the college was in Quay Street, in central Manchester, but it soon outgrew the building, and a new college was built on Oxford Street. The architect was Alfred Waterhouse, who designed so many of Manchester's buildings, and the college opened to students in 1873. Owen's College was one of the first in England to hold classes for females (but not in mixed classes), and the first to have an engineering laboratory. In 1898 when Parliament passed an Act for Manchester to have its own university, it was Owen's College which became the core of that university.

The second motorcar engine built by Henry Royce is in the North Western Museum of Science and Industry in Grosvenor Street. Henry Royce (1863-1933) built his first car in 1904 at his electrical engineering business in Cooke Street, before forming his famous partnership with C S Rolls in 1906.

MANCHESTER

A MISCELLANY

This aerial view (below) of the Barton Swing Aqueduct and the Barton Swing Road Bridge shows them both swung to let a large cargo ship through. The cargo ship has tugs fore and aft to guide it through this section of the canal. Normal operating practice is for the bridge and aqueduct to be swung clear of the Ship Canal approximately 30 minutes before a ship is due to pass through; the reason is that in the event of a failure of the operating mechanisms, there would be time to bring the ship to a halt.

MANCHESTER, THE SHIP CANAL c1965 M21505

39

MANCHESTER, MARKET STREET
1889 21900

SPORTING MANCHESTER

The grounds of Lancashire County Cricket Club and Manchester United Football Club are both called Old Trafford, after the ancestral lands of the Trafford family on which they stand.

Greyhound racing was introduced to Britain at Bellevue, in Manchester, in 1926.

The pavilion at Old Trafford cricket ground is unusual, in that it is sided to the south of the square, rather than at the end. During the First World War the pavilion was put at the disposal of the Red Cross, and over 1,800 patients were treated there over the course of the war.

It is odd that, although Manchester is universally known for its football teams, the city helped to bring about the birth of rugby. William Webb Ellis, the boy who famously 'caught the ball and ran with it' during a football match at Rugby School in 1823, was born in Salford in 1806.

Manchester-born Sunny Lowry holds the distinction of being the first English woman to swim the English Channel. She started long-distance swimming on Lake Windermere, and later in Colwyn Bay. She made two unsuccessful attempts to swim the Channel before achieving success on 28 August 1933. The swim took her 15 hours 41 minutes.

Manchester is the proud home of two successful football clubs. Maine Road, the old home of Manchester City FC, holds the records as the venue for the highest attendance in the FA Cup (apart from the final) and also in the Football League. However the FA Cup record is for a Manchester City game against Stoke on 3 March 1934, whilst the League record is for a Manchester United against Arsenal game in 1948. United were playing at Maine Road after the Second World War, after bomb damage at their own ground at Old Trafford.

Manchester Wheelers Cycling Club has been the base for many successful cyclists, including World Champion Reg Harris, and Olympic gold medallist Chris Boardman. It had a spectacular beginning on 1 June 1883. A huge meet of cycling clubs attracted a crowd of 50,000 spectators, and inspired the setting up of the Manchester Athletic Bicycle Club, later to become Manchester Wheelers.

QUIZ QUESTIONS

Answers on page 49.

1. What is the connection between Manchester and bananas?

2. Who were the Manchester Rebels?

3. Which novel by Mrs Elizabeth Gaskell features the experiences of Margaret Hale in Manchester, with the city disguised under which fictional name?

4. Manchester's City Art Gallery has a wonderful collection of the work of which famous local artist?

5. By 1842 Manchester had its own coat of arms, a crest and a motto - 'Concilio et Labore'. What does the motto mean?

6. What is the Mancunian Way?

7. Which 'first' occurred in Manchester in 1952?

8. What is the link between Manchester and old age pensions?

9. What important event happened in 1764, which transformed Manchester's fortunes?

10. What was the Peterloo Massacre?

RECIPE

MANCHESTER PUDDING

Ingredients:

Shortcrust pastry

2oz/50g butter

1oz/25g caster sugar

Rind of one lemon

Jam - any flavour of choice

2 eggs, separated into yolks and whites

1 tablespoon brandy

½ pint/300ml milk

2oz/50g fresh white breadcrumbs

Bring the milk to the boil with the lemon rind in the pan, and simmer for 5 minutes, to infuse the flavour. Remove lemon rind, and pour the milk over the breadcrumbs in a bowl. Leave to cool for 5 minutes, then beat the egg yolks into the breadcrumb mixture with the butter, sugar and brandy. Line a pie dish with pastry, and spread the base with jam. Cover with the breadcrumb mixture and bake in a moderate oven for 45 minutes. Whip the egg whites until stiff, fold in a little caster sugar and cover the pudding. Return to the oven for one minute, until the top has set. Traditionally served cold.

MANCHESTER, THE ART GALLERY AND MOSLEY STREET 1885 18285

**MANCHESTER, OWEN'S COLLEGE,
OXFORD ROAD 1895** 36350

RECIPE

LANCASHIRE PARKIN

Parkin was traditionally eaten on Bonfire, or Guy Fawkes', Night on 5 November, but its older tradition is associated with the feast days marking the beginning of winter, around the time of All Saints', or All Hallow's, Day on 1 November, and All Soul's Day on 2 November. These Christian feast days themselves have origins in the ancient Celtic feast of the dead called Samhain. Lancashire parkin came to be called 'Harcake' or 'Soul Hars Cake', and would be offered to visitors on All Saints' Day.

Ingredients:

6oz/175g plain flour

1 teaspoon salt

1 teaspoon ground ginger

2 teaspoons ground cinnamon

1 teaspoon bicarbonate of soda

10oz/275g medium oatmeal

6oz/175g black treacle

5oz/145g butter

4oz/115g dark soft brown sugar

¼ pint/150ml milk

1 egg

Sift together the flour, salt, spices and soda. Add the oatmeal and mix. Warm the treacle, butter, sugar and milk together until the butter has melted. Cool lightly, add egg and beat well. Pour into the centre of the dry ingredients and stir rapidly until smooth. Turn into a greased and lined 7-inch-square tin. Bake at 350 degrees F, 180 degrees C, Gas Mark 4, for one hour. Store in an airtight tin, and keep for a few days - two weeks is best! - before eating.

MANCHESTER, BROOKS BANK
c1873 8289

QUIZ ANSWERS

1. In 1902 Elder & Fyffe, in association with the United Fruit Co, moved their operations to Manchester, and for a few years it was the country's leading banana port.

2. On 30 November 1745, in St Anne's Square, Bonnie Prince Charlie declared his father to be King James III. James was the Roman Catholic son of King James II and was known as the 'Old Pretender', attempting to restore the Stuart succession. Prince Charles Edward Stuart then reviewed his new recruits, who later became known as the Manchester Rebels.

3. 'North and South', in which Manchester is called Milton. Mrs Gaskell knew Manchester well, as she was the wife of William Gaskell, the Unitarian minister of Cross Street Chapel.

4. L S Lowry. Manchester's City Art Gallery was one of the first supporters of this artist, who is famous for his 'matchstick men' and scenes of industrial life.

5. 'By Council and Work'.

6. The Mancunian Way is an impressive fly-over, nearly three-quarters of a mile long, that straddles the city centre from east to west.

7. In 1952 the first 'smokeless-zone' regulations in Britain were introduced in Manchester.

8. The Chancellor of the Exchequer who introduced Old Age Pensions, David Lloyd George, although of Welsh parentage, was born in Manchester in 1863.

9. The Duke of Bridgewater brought Britain's first cross-country canal into Manchester in 1764.

10. A black event in Manchester's history, which took place in 1819 on St Peter's Field, where St Peter's Square is now. During a period of industrial depression, high unemployment and great poverty, 50,000 people assembled in St Peter's Field for a political meeting. The meeting was broken up by mounted troopers with drawn sabres; eleven people were killed and hundreds were injured in what became known as the Peterloo Massacre (a reference to the Battle of Waterloo which had been fought four years earlier).

MANCHESTER, THE ROYAL JUBILEE EXHIBITION, THE ROYAL ENTRANCE 1887 21901

To celebrate Queen Victoria's Golden Jubilee in 1887 it was decided to hold an exhibition featuring Manchester's business, commerce and industry. A 32-acre site adjoining the Botanical Gardens at Old Trafford was chosen, as it had both rail and tramway connections. This photograph shows the Royal Entrance to the exhibition, which was opened by the Prince of Wales on 3 May 1887 (note the mock-up of the cathedral tower inside the exhibition ground). The exhibition ran for six months and attracted 4.75 million visitors.

FRANCIS FRITH

PIONEER VICTORIAN PHOTOGRAPHER

Francis Frith, founder of the world-famous photographic archive, was a complex and multi-talented man. A devout Quaker and a highly successful Victorian businessman, he was philosophical by nature and pioneering in outlook. By 1855 he had already established a wholesale grocery business in Liverpool, and sold it for the astonishing sum of £200,000, which is the equivalent today of over £15,000,000. Now in his thirties, and captivated by the new science of photography, Frith set out on a series of pioneering journeys up the Nile and to the Near East.

INTRIGUE AND EXPLORATION

He was the first photographer to venture beyond the sixth cataract of the Nile. Africa was still the mysterious 'Dark Continent', and Stanley and Livingstone's historic meeting was a decade into the future. The conditions for picture taking confound belief. He laboured for hours in his wicker dark-room in the sweltering heat of the desert, while the volatile chemicals fizzed dangerously in their trays. Back in London he exhibited his photographs and was 'rapturously cheered' by members of the Royal Society. His reputation as a photographer was made overnight.

VENTURE OF A LIFE-TIME

By the 1870s the railways had threaded their way across the country, and Bank Holidays and half-day Saturdays had been made obligatory by Act of Parliament. All of a sudden the working man and his family were able to enjoy days out, take holidays, and see a little more of the world.

With typical business acumen, Francis Frith foresaw that these new tourists would enjoy having souvenirs to commemorate their days out. For the next thirty years he travelled the country by train and by pony and trap, producing fine photographs of seaside resorts and beauty spots that were keenly bought by millions of Victorians. These prints were painstakingly pasted into family albums and pored over during the dark nights of winter, rekindling precious memories of summer excursions. Frith's studio was soon supplying retail shops all over the country, and by 1890 F Frith & Co had become the greatest specialist photographic publishing company in the world, with over 2,000 sales outlets, and pioneered the picture postcard.

FRANCIS FRITH'S LEGACY

Francis Frith had died in 1898 at his villa in Cannes, his great project still growing. By 1970 the archive he created contained over a third of a million pictures showing 7,000 British towns and villages.

Frith's legacy to us today is of immense significance and value, for the magnificent archive of evocative photographs he created provides a unique record of change in the cities, towns and villages throughout Britain over a century and more. Frith and his fellow studio photographers revisited locations many times down the years to update their views, compiling for us an enthralling and colourful pageant of British life and character.

We are fortunate that Frith was dedicated to recording the minutiae of everyday life. For it is this sheer wealth of visual data, the painstaking chronicle of changes in dress, transport, street layouts, buildings, housing and landscape that captivates us so much today, offering us a powerful link with the past and with the lives of our ancestors.

Computers have now made it possible for Frith's many thousands of images to be accessed almost instantly. The archive offers every one of us an opportunity to examine the places where we and our families have lived and worked down the years. Its images, depicting our shared past, are now bringing pleasure and enlightenment to millions around the world a century and more after his death.

For further information visit: www.francisfrith.com

INTERIOR DECORATION

Frith's photographs can be seen framed and as giant wall murals in thousands of pubs, restaurants, hotels, banks, retail stores and other public buildings throughout Britain. These provide interesting and attractive décor, generating strong local interest and acting as a powerful reminder of gentler days in our increasingly busy and frenetic world.

FRITH PRODUCTS

All Frith photographs are available as prints and posters in a variety of different sizes and styles. In the UK we also offer a range of other gift and stationery products illustrated with Frith photographs, although many of these are not available for delivery outside the UK – see our web site for more information on the products available for delivery in your country.

THE INTERNET

Over 100,000 photographs of Britain can be viewed and purchased on the Frith web site. The web site also includes memories and reminiscences contributed by our customers, who have personal knowledge of localities and of the people and properties depicted in Frith photographs. If you wish to learn more about a specific town or village you may find these reminiscences fascinating to browse. Why not add your own comments if you think they would be of interest to others? See **www.francisfrith.com**

PLEASE HELP US BRING FRITH'S PHOTOGRAPHS TO LIFE

Our authors do their best to recount the history of the places they write about. They give insights into how particular towns and villages developed, they describe the architecture of streets and buildings, and they discuss the lives of famous people who lived there. But however knowledgeable our authors are, the story they tell is necessarily incomplete.

Frith's photographs are so much more than plain historical documents. They are living proofs of the flow of human life down the generations. They show real people at real moments in history; and each of those people is the son or daughter of someone, the brother or sister, aunt or uncle, grandfather or grandmother of someone else. All of them lived, worked and played in the streets depicted in Frith's photographs.

We would be grateful if you would give us your insights into the places shown in our photographs: the streets and buildings, the shops, businesses and industries. Post your memories of life in those streets on the Frith website: what it was like growing up there, who ran the local shop and what shopping was like years ago; if your workplace is shown tell us about your working day and what the building is used for now. Read other visitors' memories and reconnect with your shared local history and heritage. With your help more and more Frith photographs can be brought to life, and vital memories preserved for posterity, and for the benefit of historians in the future.

Wherever possible, we will try to include some of your comments in future editions of our books. Moreover, if you spot errors in dates, titles or other facts, please let us know, because our archive records are not always completely accurate—they rely on 140 years of human endeavour and hand-compiled records. You can email us using the contact form on the website.

Thank you!

For further information, trade, or author enquiries
please contact us at the address below:

**The Francis Frith Collection, Oakley Business Park,
Wylye Road, Dinton, Wiltshire SP3 5EU.**
Tel: +44 (0)1722 716 376 Fax: +44 (0)1722 716 881
e-mail: sales@francisfrith.co.uk **www.francisfrith.com**